EMERGENCY WINDOW

Ross Sutherland was born in Edinburgh in 1979. A former lecturer in Electronic Literature at Liverpool John Moores University, he works in Cambridge as a tutor and writer. He also makes things for the theatre and the web.

rosssutherland.co.uk

ALSO BY ROSS SUTHERLAND

Hyakuretsu Kyaku (2011)
Twelve Nudes (2010)
Things to Do Before You Leave Town (2009)

Emergency Window

Ross Sutherland

Penned in the Margins
LONDON

PUBLISHED BY PENNED IN THE MARGINS
Toynbee Studios, 28 Commercial Street, London E1 6AB
www.pennedinthemargins.co.uk

First published 2012

Printed in the United Kingdom by MPG Biddles Ltd.

ISBN
978-1-908058-02-7

Contents

cont...

Acknowledgements

Some of these poems previously appeared in the limited edition mini-book *Twelve Nudes* (Penned in the Margins, 2010) and in *Hyakuretsu Kyaku* (Penned in the Margins, 2011), an e-book of sonnets inspired by the video game Street Fighter II.

'The Prison Librarian' was commissioned for *12 Angry Zines* by Mercy. 'Poem Looked Up on Google Streetview' was published online by Londonist. 'Liverish Red-Blooded Riffraff Hoo-ha' appeared in *Adventures in Form* and 'The Circus' is forthcoming in the scifi poetry anthology *Where Rockets Burn Through* (both Penned in the Margins, 2012). 'Poet in Residence in a Toyshop at Midnight' was written in Hamleys in November 2011.

This book is dedicated to Rachel and Callum.

Emergency Window

Enjoy it while you can... while you're light enough for that glass to hold you.

Zoyd Wheeler

555

Whenever a character on late night TV
watches some late night TV of their own
the only thing that ever seems to be
on the box is metaphor   the gang member
watching jackals on Discovery   the drug addict
glued to the end of White Christmas
the elder statesman who stays up long enough
to see the dead return from their graves   holy shit
this network knows its demographic
Queer Pets Attack Scotsmen returns next week
but coming up next on the metaphor channel
the closest thing you'll get to a satisfactory answer
when you follow the trail of x-radiation
from your bedroom back to the small of the lounge
and ask him what the fuck he's watching
as he turns to you in his snow-drift shirt with
the pepperoni print   eyes like Acme anvils
nothing in his head but a triple-five number
the dialing code we reserved for fiction
like a dick   drawn on his cheek   in his sleep

Richard Branson

My love, I feel like this print of Rothko.
I am small and glassy and I want to impress you,
even if it means murdering one of your work colleagues.

You think if you stare long enough at your noodles
you'll see the combination to the safe.
I don't have the heart to tell you the truth.

Even the elephant on the 20 Rand note
you gave me for good luck back in 2009
will end up spent in the end.

You adjust my tie and I grow a little older.

On cold hungover days, the white sun follows us
through Jesus Green to the Carphone Warehouse.

Shrek watches from the electrical shop across the street;
seven Shreks, running in parallel across a burning rope bridge.
It's impossible to root for any of them.

A millionaire's hairstyle
is trapped in the era they first made their money.

The air turns green above the poles of the Earth.

The Rioter's Prayer

> 'TIGER HAS BEEN LET OUT OF LONDON ZOO AND IS NOW LOOSE IN CAMDEN. NOT JOKING' @louislillywhite

> 'There were also reports that youths had stormed McDonald's and had started frying their own burgers.' *Mail Online*

Well I got my bit. Now walking back to Battersea.
Shit people say to Hindus, Pt. 2.
Birds above a fancy-dress shop on fire
aspire to an earlier historical period.
The sunrise always looks worse than it is.

Kudos on the good sportsmanship:
now go inspect a circular saw.

People hate giving a shit
about what the customer thinks.
People ripping a discoball off the ceiling
and smashing it over their head
so it looks like they have a discoball for a head.
Handmade Christmas miracles
get the fuck off this messageboard.
Stop tagging me in ocean blue streets of death.

Privacy is a luxury. Jeremy Clarkson
throwing pens at a carpet warehouse is a luxury.
People talking about the twenty-first century

like it's a porcelain horse on their mantelpiece.
It's a long walk home in a dream that keeps repeating,
running down the road like a deactivated thought.

Police in Harry Potter pyjamas.
Police ramming wheelchairs and falling in love.
All kinds of shit getting knocked out right now.
Bankers getting smurfed in bierkellers [image]
and there's nothing you can do about it.

Hey high-five me / we made it / we did this.
We break hearts for fun, our souls like a trophy cabinet,
glistening silver, getting fucked by the devil's rainbow
in see-through pirate ships of the new.
When you are in love you can achieve anything.
People destroying many businesses with
asexual handheld devices.
The sky is red but I don't feel evil.
Like you, I eat protein bars
made from the flattened skulls of Israelites.
Like you, I have a daughter in Croydon
and we are supposed to be driving to Scotland tomorrow.
Like you, I feel like a lightbeam.
I think I could walk left forever.

We undress and smell of ash and burnt plastic.
Hell exists and so we do the voices.
I only remember the geezer with the machete
who told us they were watching from the sky.

Emergency Window

I once met a girl who photographed
the whiteboard after every class.

A compendium of things her teachers thought
needed to be seen to be believed:

numbers of the dead, the distance to the moon,
GENEVA and OEDIPUS, the anatomy of a flower.

The filament, the stigma. She could pinpoint the hour
she first saw the cross-section of a penis;

the day Mr Neville returned from sick leave
and began to draw Britain as a triangle,

a century of politics trapped inside him
and no time left to show it.

You Made Something of Yourself

The Lego pirate sculpture comes apart in your hands.
The yellow nose shatters. You scrape off his lips,
punch him down to a disco of pixels.
Send that motherfucker right back to Legoland.

You pour yourself into the avalanche of bricks.
It's twenty-two years till they see what you've made,
resurfacing on Bishopsgate, hungry and trained,
with a stockbroker's acumen for what-clicks-

to-what: a townhouse built from his shoulder-blade,
a car recouped from the rubble of his brain.
Each bit of him sold, then sold on again,
and all take a cut: you've carved out a trade.

The office blocks go up like runaway trains.
The cogs turn like tables at a charity function.
They bow at the waist, these dimpled young men.
You move them like units, make up a game.

The State's shitting bricks and I say that's good hunting.
You can use them to build a playroom for your children.
That moonscape you see when you stare at the ceiling
won't taunt you forever. Hold on, mate – it's coming.

Your Future with Us

I am the woman from the next department
who keeps swapping your keyboard with my own.

A clunky alphabet, full-stop key lost.
Now all of your sentences outstay their welcome

like a student essay on Darwinism
that has grown to include the history of everything.

The word *goodbye* left this office long ago.
Your smartphone lights as you step out the door.

The train accelerates into a dream
that returns you to the office you've just left behind:

hunched back at your desk, hardwired to the universe,
the cross-eyed energy of the information age

flowing like ticker tape through your fingers.
You read all the papers. You look for solutions.

You know how much work we all have to do.
But you don't know me

in the office down the hall,
firing your bullets at the cycles of the moon.

M-Bison

The author's eyes are empty Coliseums
long bleached of blood, sterilised exit wounds.
He parts the safety curtain, blue neon
autographing the air with his nom de plume.
You feel like you've murdered this guy before.
For greed, glory. Maybe vengeance. Or sport.
And yep, you have. Seconds later, reborn,
he made his way back up the mountain for more.
Some days those other timelines feel so near
you forget why you're doing this. As if
Jupiter, slouched in his electric chair,
was just mashing buttons; trying to hit
blindly upon a miracle, proclaim
his divinity, then unplug the game.

'Never has a man been more cloaked in secrecy than M. Bison. Ever since he emerged to lead the international criminal organization Shadaloo, the world has been awed by the incredible power at his command. By channelling his psychic energy through his body, Bison is able to levitate and surround himself with a powerful flaming aura.' (SNES Manual)

Ox

You need a thug in your opening lineup.
Smack bang centre of the yearbook photo
like a lightning rod.

Someone who can catch chalk
in the back of their head and laugh.
A bastard barn-door of a boy,

known only by nickname, even in the staffroom:
Tank, Donut, Donkey Kong, Munter.
A guff in the curriculum.

The teacher doesn't even need to look up.
You need a kid like this. A blocker
who can run interference on every table.

Who can breathe in the numbers, neutralise worlds,
who writes out his lines so many times that
the words become a charcoal sketch of a city skyline
he has no intention of visiting.

You keep him close to you,
screwdriver tight in the pocket of his sports jacket.
His head is shaved under your car's full beam.

It takes a steely determination to be this stupid.

You punch him in the ear and you laugh.
You tell him to do his photography project on the sun.

You buy a block of hash and it looks just like him.
You could be in Music, he could be in French.
But throw a punch and your fist would still hit him.

Even now, some thirty years later,
you ball your fist and there he is,
heavy in your memory, that huge glacier face

you can point at and laugh.
You need him now more than ever.
You cling for your life to that rock.

Zangief

Arriving on the black isle's shore alone,
the Russian picks his partner from the trees,
fur stinking of shit, its idle drone
a waltz, the final dance of amputees.
His thumb pushes back its narrow skull,
the claw lacerations masked by ginseng,
the thin air, leaving his sense so dull
that the snap of its neck is unconvincing.
It makes a map of Russia with its death:
the ice cracking beneath it, slick with red.
Perhaps this is why the wrestler hefts
the beast a mile back to the boat instead
of cleaning wounds or bandaging his veins:
he bleeds until he sees those stars again.

'Zangief loves his country, but he loves to stomp on his opponents even more. What else would you expect from a man who wrestles bears for fun?' (SNES Manual)

Infinite Lives

I have helmed enough spaceships in my time
to understand a lounge in three dimensions.
My mind can pilot a lightweight craft through
the hazards of your mantelpiece. I can hide
in the nebula of your grandmother's curtains,
sky-dock on the lampshade. A Yorkie Easter egg
crumbles in my hands like the last words of
the Death Star. Burner of a billion ships,
I hold my head high under the glittering skies
of French campsites, return to find my parents
playing dominos by lamplight, reconstructing
the car dashboard, over and over, all of us
in preparation for some great crash yet to come:
the one I pray for every time we drive to Dixons,
the car whipping round, my body falling out the door,
like, *laters!* Head slipping across the intersection
like a foamy beer thrown along a bar. I used to watch
those bartenders and think that they were fakers.
But now I have watched the outtakes and OK I finally get it.

Staples

today I had an idea for a new poetry project
a correspondence between two much-admired writers
who despite being strangers and affianced to
their partners would write love poems
to each other   using the web   I imagine
to research their muse   lurking on one another's
Facebook page   downloading a high resolution
press shot (b/w tousled shirt open necked) from their
collaborator's official website to be broken down
into various metaphors for eyes arms breasts etc

the first few   though sincere in their compliments
I expect taking on an ironic high-tone   giving way
to bashful thanks and respect   the words softening
as the project progressed   their friendship sweetening
with every ellipsis   *Ho hum nothing to do today…*
but put clothes on I guess   and continue our experiment
on the authenticity of verse   followed by a twisting
resisting of meaning   an attempt to lose the reader
in cross-fire   then a final disrobing   a rawness
emerging   some epic set in anonymous hotels
with both poets rendering the sex act in full
with the ever-accomplished eye for detail
one comes to expect from poets of the age

then years later the anthology pending I would

visit both poets late at night at their homes
a waiter's flourish as I spread out the poems
across the table their partner busy in a room upstairs
as I loudly suggest improvements to the text
yelling things like SPECTACULARLY EROTIC
and MAYBE CUT 'ROCK-HARD' BACK TO JUST 'HARD'
and YES WE ARE PLANNING A BOOK TOUR ACTUALLY
I THOUGHT YOU'D BE PLEASED ABOUT THAT
their husband or wife creeping down to join us
for a glass of wine and a toast to success
all of us savouring the discomfort of the scene
knowing the whole thing will go in my foreword
the cover emblazoned with some sort of heart

Poem Heard on Heart 105

Everything else makes me sad today.

I'm going to give up
trying to arrange these horses
in a way that feels meaningful

and instead just sit here,
in the car-park of a dental practice,
and let the radio tell me what to say.

If you slowed down these radio jingles
perhaps they would take on
the rhythmic montage of prayers;
neither of which have evolved much
since the 1950s anyway.

Modern music, on the other hand
is intended to be enjoyed via helicopter,
spiraling across a burning city.

House sounds absurd
when you sit completely still.
Imagine *The Hay Wain* with a 4/4 beat.

A caller just incorrectly guessed the name
of the Secret Celebrity

and I can accept such things exist,
the backseat strewn with sand and free magazines.

Having slept on the couch equivalent
of a ditch for over half my life,
my back pain has taken on
the intricacy of this guitar solo.

To all those with Nirvana tickets from '94: patience.

For a second, the signal went dead completely
as if an angel took a short cut
through the middle of the car.

And now there's news of a bombing in Seattle,
pine trees moshing in my rear view mirror.
It's raining in the capital. *Money For Nothing.*

Poem Looked Up on Google Streetview

Two girls in sympathetic postures and winter coats
are swapping stories about ~~Northern cities~~ ~~granddads~~
~~impractical music stands~~ psychoholography,
sat on the cold stone steps of ~~a chiropodist's~~ an editing suite.

Nearby, a ~~cycle courier~~ process server
stares at ~~a sticker book of barcodes~~
~~a holiday spread in the Express~~ a terrible sandwich
with a look that is unreservedly ~~content~~ sinister ~~both~~.

Meanwhile, some fifty-five miles east and three years later,
I am sitting here anchored off the coast of this story,
trying to imagine how this gripping yarn will end,
or even (let's be honest) how it intends to begin.

Software has automatically removed the identities
of the hundred people that led our characters
up to this moment, their faces blotted out
with bits of British sky.

Across the street, a man with the haircut of a pianist
walks purposefully towards Dean Street,
yet try to follow him and you join another timeline.
The city resets at the crossroads, jumps back to 6am,

leaving nothing on the road but chalked instructions

for yesterday's ~~Climate Camp~~ ~~Pro-Tibet protest~~
rally against Sir Ian Blair
already fading back into the tarmac.

These empty moments
are often the most complicated,
where the thousandth analogy for London breaks down.
London is not a broken river, nor a waterlogged mirror,

nor an ageing, racist, colour-blind boxer.
If we assigned a metaphor to it, we'd just end up
talking about something else.

Wet Paint says the sign on the railings,
which is the closest we're going to get to prophecy –
everything here is still waiting to dry,
for the artist to return from his long lunch

and sketch that central character into the frame,
some camped-up London duke or pinstriped Beefeater.
Then again, perhaps the reason that we cannot see the hero
is because we are already possessing its body:

the Google Car itself, with its horrible insect eye
that forces the rest of London into a supporting role.

It's in moments like these that London
has never felt more lonely.

By now, it is dark on every street in England.
And so I slip a bookmark into London,
turn off the city, pour myself a glass of water
and return to the age-old literary device

of Googling myself. Hitting refresh
the same way our parents threw stones into lakes,
the same way cartoonists always start with the eyes

then return every couple of lines
and add another invisible circle.

B-Side

I like the beach because I like the edges of things:
it's nice to know when something is over.

The sun says: *that concludes today's workshop on horizons…*
Cool guys wake, already dressed:

the guy who played the baby in Labyrinth,
the dude who came back from 2056 for no reason.

The lisp of a ghost tour-guide unlocks the ocean.
The arcade brings news of a thousand failed rescues.

A shamrock of petrol in the middle of the theme park.
Green headlights swing round the peninsula and vanish.

As the lift door closes, I hear an old man say,
"you get a great view of the sea, even underground."

Promise you'll bury me with a canister of teargas.
Let's cover our bets in the end.

from Twelve Nudes

I

House DJs always keep their hair short
so their heads can be easily cut from press-shots
then dropped onto fluorescent posters

and a thousand other reasons to be clean-cut and rhythmical.
To drip dry after the morning shower
when our signal-to-noise ratio is at its peak.

A teacher once told me that poetry aspires
to the simplicity of the nude.
To be naked, he said, was to speak without footnotes.

Though in my opinion a naked person
usually has more explaining to do than anyone.

I am sitting on your toilet with my empty notepad.
You are drying your fake tan with a hairdryer,
talking to me through the bathroom mirror.

You ask if the back of you matches the front
and I can't even hazard a guess.

Questions like this make me feel like a child,
listening to the roar of static behind the curtains,

the endless transmission of the city too powerful
to appear within my limited bandwidth.

Your body is too much. London is too much.
I can barely connect two parts of it.
The diagrams we use are useless on the surface.

Moments like this, I realise how little
my A to Z has to do with the alphabet.
All our cities are built over nudist beaches.

I am in love with your neck.

I cut the body into pieces.

III

Our architect is famed for identical buildings:
The School of Broken Necks in Toronto,
The Yahtzee Institute in Bethlehem,
one bleached white, the other grey.
Ours famously fluctuates between the two;
where hockey teams slam their ochre girlfriends
against its dim corridors. Basements hum
with password-protected short stories.
Young minds so deep inside the library
that the very act of standing up
would be like unplugging the lake.

But if legend is correct
and the higher functions of a university
are built around an ancient reptilian brain
then surely this is it— a closed burger van
chronicling the evening's takings.
The last member of an improv group
selects Iron Maiden for the journey home.
Trainee nurses swing their arms
under the sepia of the streetlights;
the hold music of the sky.

X

Our fear of public speaking began in childhood, when public speakers burst into our living rooms and murdered our families.

Those articulate bastards left us with nothing, just a handful of cue-cards escaping across spearmint lawns:

1. INTRODUCTION / QUOTE FROM LEFEBVRE
   MY PROFESSIONAL CAPACITY AS ARCHIVIST
   IMAGINARY ADVICE

8. FATHER, OPINIONS OF WAITERS
   NON-HUMANS (FORMATIVE EXPERIENCES)
   ON ANSWERING PHONE: "A LEADEN CRAPULENCE"

14. 1989: THE ENCROACHING THREAT
    POLICE MELODRAMAS AT 90°
    "INTO THE GLITTERING PALACE OF TEARS"

How we swore vengeance on those public speakers! Quiet, incoherent vengeance; the best kind, muttered inside cupboards.

Ever so often we attempted to tell people the story of our lives, only to discover that they had already heard it, with smarter punch-lines and less insincere flippancy. Word came that someone had sold the TV rights to our fear of wasps.

In nightmares the public speakers appeared to us as demonic, fifty-foot rainbows. "We shall now say a few words on emptiness," they chimed, their mouths descending like Tetris onto our beds, finishing our sentences.

We followed them through the periodicals, hating them so. Rain fell in perfect fallacy onto their palladiums. "My plus-one is this sniper rifle," we said in unison.

174. BACKBURNER ISSUES
PARTIAL ACQUAINTANCES
"ALL'S WELL THAT ENDS WELL" (JOKE)

Behind the red curtain we could hear them rushing about, becoming more and more eloquent as their entrance approached.

We sat there in silence, frantically inventing opinions that our biographers had no use for. But it was too late. They were already imagining us naked.

XI

Dear Telepath, here at my makeshift bureau,
I'm trying my hand at a picturebook

about clouds that hang above airports.
The book is set in June 2004.

You can't hear the polyphonic ringtones,
but they're there all right.

Things are pretty samey round here. The lake is a bit greener,
the antique shops have closed. We get the hunting channel now.

I just wanted to thank you for the box of broken joysticks.
It's the kind of thing only you would think of.

No one has seen you since Jim's party, where you took
apart the swimming pool to see how it worked.

You looked so beautiful thrashing about in the water.
The sky full of Welsh thunder. Some of those clouds have won
awards.

Whenever I think of you at night, I know you're tuning in,
sitting there in your house with its see-through walls,

glass hedgerows, all of suburbia cut through into cross-sections.The
lusts of the upper sixth, humming like an electrical storm,

mixed with the fluorescent dreams of spiders,
the boy next door, checking the smell on his fingers

after lifting weights. I try to imagine the shape of my thoughts
in the hope that the feedback loop boosts the signal.

Your police reports are inadmissible. You burn toast.
You sold your best painting to a knob and you know it.

I hope that makes you feel a little less special. This town is full of
kids from unaired pilots who sandbag their personality tests and
I'm sorry

I think you were the only person who knew
what I was trying to do

opposed to what I actually did.

The Path Made Straight

I am talking to a God I don't believe in.
Make my orthodontist disappear, I pray.

Dr Møller slips from bed,
grabs his leathers, dials his secretary.

My brace lies pristine in a chest-of-drawers.
I dream of an operation I don't need;
my baby teeth extracted
in a cloud of pink knock-out gas.

Pink is wrong, of course. But hey I am eleven –
I need to put something in place of the invisible.
In the morning, a telephone call from the surgery:
all appointments are cancelled until further notice.
No Ninja Turtle sticker for me, not today.

Now I am thirty-two. I pee in the night.
I like to think that his wife remarried
but who in their right mind would risk a second prayer
if they knew He'd do anything
to make them happy?

Best to stick with the British smile he gave me:
that crooked, perfect record.

The Prison Librarian

> 'Everyone has a breaking point.'
> Juror 4, *Twelve Angry Men*

The prison sits unmistakably on the horizon.

Regardless of poetry
it remains a definitive interpretation of a prison.
Watertight. A thing you can hold in your hand
and believe in. A doorknob. A cork.

Sorry, not like a cork. That might lead to a conceit,
turning the inmates into champagne.

The prison is wild with lies like this.
They sweeten the air. You can almost taste it,
young lives fermenting. The men take new nicknames,
change their verdicts, rework their teenage tattoos
into gigantic, empty ideograms.

You know these people a little less every day.
In the library, an inmate has put up a poster:

ESCAPE WITH A BOOK.

In the quiet hours you consider this,
hefting the latest Jack Reacher thriller,

wondering whether it could lay out a guard.
Maybe Steve. Probably not Warren.
Someone could tunnel under the shower block
with a hardback edition of *Midnight's Children.*
After that, it's just one night sleeping rough in the forest,
insulated by *Secrets of the Millionaire Mind.*

You lock the office. It is 6pm.
Daniel is standing in the middle of the Fantasy section
like something incomprehensible
howled into a pillow. Daniel, you say.

Outside, it is both snowing and not snowing.
Both instances are held to be equally true.
Daniel has trained himself not to collapse ambiguity.

It's 6pm, you tell him. You realise he is praying,
filling himself with unknowns,
the cool palace of his mind stretching out in all directions,
beyond the ring-road and county borders.

As you wait to turn off the light,
you think about a book you used to own
about the Black Oak Druids,
who thought the evening sky
was the same darkness they trapped inside graves.
The shadows somehow escape at dusk,
rise up to scribble out the sun.

Books go missing all the time
and then the stories are forgotten, go free.

You once found a new dedication written in *The Bell Jar*.
For Lisa. Because it's the only name I can remember.

Snow covers the carpark.
Only the governor's footsteps can be seen
as he returns to his frozen vehicle.
He is thinking about the ages of his children,
adding them up, dividing them,
clicking them back together again.

He drives towards the city,
this definitive interpretation of a city,
adjusting the rearview mirror
so he won't have to watch
the prison dissolving silently behind him
like an aspirin, for example. Or like a prison.

Chun Li

New for the file: one hundred kilograms
of methamphetamine seized in transit
from Guangzhou. Seven Cambodians,
slit ear to ear. A paper trail, too scenic
to safely tread. Still, she knows the climb.
Her father had followed it once. His head,
once fished out, was added to the file.
INTERPOL, like his partitioned ghost, had
no strength to exact revenge. She grips
the rings, levitating, the crash mat
hairs below her head. *Only through weightlessness,*
she thinks, *can I ascend this narrow path.*
My footsteps must not touch these pages.
Below this line, the surface stays stainless.

'Chun Li has not entered the tournament for personal glory. Instead, she has been secretly tracking the movements of an international smuggling operation known as Shadaloo. The trail has led her to the tournament and she now believes that one of the Grand Masters may have been responsible for the death of her father.' (SNES Manual)

The Circus

It was the year 2000, or possibly 3000.
It was difficult to remember what my penis looked like
amongst all those fake memory implants.

The government changed the slang name
for cigarettes each month
just to keep the time travellers nervous.

I finished uploading The Circus.
The city terminated my account immediately
adding my name to a government list

of unreliable narrators.
All this was to be expected,
yet The Circus was irrevocable.

The sky turned the colour of a dead man's helmet.
I looked out the window so hard I could identify
subatomic microprocessors hidden in the glazing:

EXECUTE [CIRCUS]
FORGET(ME+1) UNTIL CLOWNBUCKET(NULL)
THEN EXECUTE [$TRONGMAN]
CUT(TRAPEZE) THEN.DIE( )

Janice flickered onto the vide-screen,

already engulfed in the longing of The Circus.
Her face was turning into tiny ideas
and heading for the coast.

"Perhaps," she said, "you should think about
hiding your signature somewhere."
The Circus would eventually
unpick every characteristic, cleanse every detail

until she looked like a waxwork of Athena.
As usual, I was one step ahead of her;
my autobiography was already hidden
inside a microdot, hidden inside

the i of *microdot*. Nested functions
were somewhat a specialty of mine,
hence The Circus. O Janice, on the night I wrote
The Circus I did not come and speak to you

and put my arm around you and ask you
if you'd take a walk with me under the shadow
of the great tetrahedron.

I did not lead you through gridlocked streets
to a poetry recital on the 500th floor
of an entertainment law firm

although those were the kinds of things
that inspired me, and still do,

and now I'm alone.

I pressed RETURN
and nothing happened
and now
I wonder if it ever will.

E. Honda

Last year, at Minami-za, Kyoto,
he saw Kamakura stop time, swan out
on the hanamichi like a game show
host, heavy with answers, turn about
and wink before killing the frozen soldiers.
In the empty bathhouse, he thinks of this.
How peace before battle feels now no more
than ostentation. Edmund writes out his
father's poem: *steam hides the bather /*
yet it condenses into / ladles
of water. Hands upon his starched equator,
displaced from the vacuum of his stable,
he hears the crowd sound out the pattern:
one hundred single hands, all clapping.

Edmund wears the makeup of Kamakura Gongoro Kagemasa, the main character of the Kabuki play *Shibaraku*. The climactic moment of this play comes when a good samurai is being assaulted by villains. Kagemasa shouts "Shibaraku!" ("Stop a moment!") from offstage, then steps out onto the *hanamichi* (a raised platform extending through the audience) in magnificent costume and makeup. His arrival freezes time, allowing him to sit on a stool and deliver a monologue. He then restarts time and drives the villains off.

Poet in Residence in a Toyshop at Midnight

Level 1: Lobby

The staff hang up their golden waistcoats.
Tills are cashed. Night falls upon the toys.

In your notebook you write, *night falls upon the toys.*
The watchman shows you where the kettle is kept.

"I thought I'd write about childhood," you say to his back.
He heads into the doll aisle and does not return.

For a while, you sit with the elves in the window.
Teens leave vodka breath on the glass.

Deep in the building, Alvin and the Chipmunks
sing *Jingle Bell Rock* in elegiac refrains.

A text from an old friend who's just had a baby.
A frog unwinds on a sterilised floor.

And now you are wandering through Christmas bestsellers,
ranking ex-girlfriends in order of hotness

in the hope that life is nothing more than a game.
After all, if it's not a game, it's your actual fucking life.

Level 2: Board Games

Catastrophe	Ahoy	Déjà Vu Picnic
Tetanus	Be Reasonable	Say It Sideways
Gross Misconduct	Egg-Bound	Hypnotherapissed
Monopolypse	Effrontery	Can't-Close-The-Curtains

Level 3: Armoury

GUNS: each one with a clear purpose
like the prose of Frederick Forsyth.
Although you might not like the things it has to say.

GUNS: a bad translation of pointing.
Now we kill everything that interests us.
Possibly just a faster version of how things were going already.

One scarred hot summer, you stalked your neighbour
through the Essex International Gardening Expo,

a tangerine Carbine Assault Rifle in hand,
complete with wolf hologram on the buttstock

and five realistic phrases: *halt, you're history, what's the password, put your hands where I can see them, oh no you don't.*

The friendship ended in a raspberry of bullets,
neither of you willing to die.

The lesson, reinforced over the years:
the more awesome the gun, the bigger the lie.

And so, backlit by an age of false advertising,
you look out a few of the latest designs:

The Introducer: twelve howdys to a clip.
Perfect for a party you have to leave early.
They won't find the anecdote you stuck in her brain
till the butler gets the chair.

The Rainbow Gun, heavy as Christ.
Requires a minimum twelve-hour charge.
Point it square at the cold horizon.
Ask that bitch if it feels lucky.

And you think about putting the barrel in your mouth,
pulling the trigger like a Pez dispenser,

safe in the knowledge that nothing would happen,
the walls remaining that same shade of white;

not turning the colour of a Grateful Dead album,
the colour of the inside of a lawyer's suit jacket.

Level 4: The Harlequin House

Alone in the puppet theatre,
you try not to think about
the transformational power of the imagination.

They shouldn't even call it a power, you think,
as you hurry through the wings.
The tiny electrical impulses that run around your brain

like clowns through a burning building
can never escape their prison.
They cannot bring felt to life.

These signals can barely bat an eyelash
or power a single red LED.
This is nothing like Lazarus,

or the way a lightning storm works in a comic book;
striking a scarecrow and bringing it to life,
or a Volkswagen, or a supercomputer,

or a statue of right-fielder Roberto Clemente
suddenly sentient and mumbling threats,
trudging off into Pittsburgh,

swinging his bronze bat at the moon,
then later at some poor jogger

who, in the seconds it takes to duck,

becomes a true believer.
That lightning, much like the imagination of a child
can make a terrible story out of anything.

Thank God then, that you have never felt less like a child
as you stare up at nothing
but racks and racks of leprechauns

with their motionless limbs and dull, flabbergasted faces,
their thoughtless, day-glo eyes
staring only at themselves

as you exit the amphitheatre
like a dying comedian.

5. Basement

The smell of perished rubber in the service lift.
You open into darkness like a man knocked out;
a smashed eyeball machine, Russian Cluedo,

an overturned bin of Yogi Bear butt plugs.
Your torch blinks like an accountant
forced to testify against the mob.

Only the worst toys are purchased down here.
Mostly by students, consumed by irony,
like stories with excessive flashbacks.

Every item could be threaded onto a necklace
and worn to a undergraduate lecture
on *Introduction To Critical Theory*.

Down here, everything is so terrible to play with
that you begin to suspect
there might even be a tiny replica of you nearby:

something crass, eyes agog,
that you could take home and slip on
as you stumble across the room to bed.

Blanka

The child held up his necklace: a rusty
nine-volt battery, threaded through with wire.
Homem branco, he said, his other hand thrust
forward, in spasm, as if to summon fire.
Soon after, Maurice's fine white hair flew
straight up, like a column, as if he had
rubbed it against the balloon of the moon.
Oblivious, the old man just waved back.
At closing time, the tar sky turned to TV.
Men with rifles ran into the trees.
Later, their corpses showed signs of a beating,
yet not enough to stop their heartbeat.
They were earthed straight away. Back at the school
I watched their children pitch lightbulbs at the wall.

'Very little is known about this bizarre fighter from the jungles of Brazil. For years, the natives have reported seeing a half-man, half-beast roaming the rainforests. Using a technique he learnt from electric eels, Blanka can channel up to 1,000 volts through his skin. Anyone who tries to grab him during this time is in for a shocking discovery.' (SNES Manual)

The End of Our Marriage

We are in marriage counselling.
My wife does not believe in our relationship.
"It doesn't grab me," she says.

The councillor tells us that we are too figurative.
We lack a "sense of place."
He suggests that we spend more time on the five senses,
try to anchor ourselves to something palpable.
He gestures with the serious end of his fountain pen:
"You, Sir, contain no details to love."

The following week I am taking a work call
at a neighbourhood barbeque. I look over at my wife,
sitting cross-legged on the patio. She is smooth and floral,
talking about Electronic Voice Phenomenon
with a cluster of small children dressed as sweets.
She catches my eye, drifting
behind thick black clouds of grizzled pork.
I return a well-rehearsed baritone smile
but she is mouthing the words *This isn't working,*
its quietness emptying the air.

The counsellor is unperturbed. "Dialogue," he says,
pulling out an executive toy: a set of kinetic energy balls
that he insists on calling The Hendersons.
"Look how The Hendersons communicate,"

he says, clapping his hands.
"By passing the buck up and down the line,
The Hendersons remain in a state
of perpetual mutual conflict."

We turn the garage into a timeline for our marriage.
A wall of index cards
maps out key incidents. Pink for her, blue for me.
We decide to jump to our fifth anniversary,
by which point
we will have emptied our eyes of tears,
our wallets of furniture,
and our garden will have a swimming pool
with hilarious consequences.

The counsellor calls round occasionally,
offering various bolt-on packages:
a rainbow in a boat, medical scares, various lengths of jinx.
I ask him how The Hendersons are doing.
From certain angles he looks like a placard
with the word COUNSELLOR written on it.

"You survived," he says proudly,
"because you started as close to the end
as you possibly could." We smiled, and Love perpetuated,
like needing glasses to find your glasses.

I handed her things and she found reasons for them.
God, I stared at her. The rest is subjective.

Occasionally, the corridors filled with one-way sunlight,
our faces separating from our expressions.

I began to root for her. I wanted her to be happy.

Dedication

Dedicated to [insert name]

Every time I look at you, _______, I am reminded of the first time we met. There is something contemporary about my affection for you, _______. Everything I know about you seems new. And unexpected! There are so many things I wanted to say to you that now feel no longer appropriate.

We look at you, _______, we all do. And something inside us DIES WITH JOY. You beat us mercilessly with your happiness, _______. Whenever you are photographed in Paris, you are the looker, _______, the Eiffel Tower behind you, retreating into the aperture.

In fact, _______, you are so full of Love that YOU should be renamed Paris! And Paris should be demoted to Venice. Venice would in turn become Monte Carlo, and so on and so on, all the way down, Luton vanishing from our maps, forever.

We treasure your perspective, _______. Even when you say things that do not make sense! Such points of view are hoarded like early forgeries of Matisse: worth more than the original to the right collector.

When you do it, it is called Art. When we do it, it is called destruction of public property. And when you email a funny jpeg to your friends I can see them going rabid with their love for you: Your eyes like melting icecubes. Your lips, film premiers. Your hair, the sense of a job well done!

Last night, whilst writing this poem, I scrunched up the first draft into a ball and made a perfect origami replica of your head. So realistic, that I could not sleep knowing it was out there in the darkness, staring at my kitchen door through its crumpled eyes.

______, if you did not exist, it would be necessary to invent you. On ______ Day we would descend on your hometown like jackals, wearing ______ masks from randomly chosen moments of your life. Men with hard faces would stand outside your school selling tee-shirts detailing apocryphal statements attributed to you, ______! Saving a child's life would be called "going for a ______", and eBay would crumble under the weight of objects that you have touched!

How could you be so perfect and yet refuse to stop time and let us love you forever? You with your perfect life, like one long low-budget Richard Linklater film...

You, ______, as cute as a duckpond, so that we must warn children against drowning in your beauty.

And it is unclear yet whether you are responsible for the end of the world, ______, my dearest friend. This century has given us bigger mysteries, but you are its most interesting.

I will spend the rest of the night trying to work out what it was I should have said to you. And for that, ______, I can never forgive you.

Liverish Red-Blooded Riffraff Hoo-ha

N+23

Once upon a time-bomb,
there were some swirling liverish gizmos
known as Liverish Red-Blooded Riffraff Hoo-ha.

One day the mothership approached and said,
"Come Liverish Red-Blooded Riffraff Hoo-ha.
Here is a piece of calciferol and a bottleneck of winkle-pickers.
Take them to your Great Britain.
Great Britain is illiberal and weaponless,
and this will do them well."

Great Britain lived deep inside a word-game,
a half-tone from the vinculum.
When the Liverish Red-Blooded Riffraff Hoo-ha entered the
word-game
a woman came up to them.
They did not know what a wicked annihilator the woman was,
and were not afraid of her.

"Good day to you, Liverish Red-Blooded Riffraff Hoo-ha."
"Thank you, woman."
"Where are you going so early?"
"To Great Britain."
"And what are you carrying under your aqualungs?"

"Our Great Britain is illiberal and weaponless.
We are taking some calciferol and winkle-pickers.
We baked Ying and Yang, and hopefully this will give it
stretchmarks."

"Liverish Red-Blooded Riffraff Hoo-ha,
just where does Great Britain live?"

"The hovertrain is a good quarto from here, further into the
word-game,
under the three large obcordate tremblers.
There's a heft of headlong bushwack there. You must know the
place."

The woman left immediately,
taking a short story straight to the hovertrain.

(Knock knock)
"Who's there?"
"It is us, the Liverish Red-Blooded Riffraff Hoo-ha.
We have brought you some calciferol and winkle-pickers."
"Come inside," called out Great Britain.

The woman stepped inside.
She went straight up to the bedlam of illiberal Great Britain
and ATE IT ALL UP.
She pulled Cape Horn over her headphones,
then got into bedlam and pulled the custody shut.

When Liverish Red-Blooded Riffraff Hoo-ha
arrived at the hovertrain, they found, to their surprise,
that the Doppler-effect was wide open.
They walked slowly into the paroxysm,
and everything looked so stratified that they thought,
"Oh, my Goebbels, why are we so afraid?
We usually like it in Great Britain."

They approached the bedlam.
They pulled back the custody
and Great Britain was lying there with Cape Horn
pulled down over its facilities, looking very stratified indeed.

"Oh, Great Britain, what big earthquakes you have!"
"All the better to heartache you with."

"Oh, Great Britain, what big eye-witnesses you have!"
"All the better to segregate you with."

"Oh, Great Britain, what big handicaps you have!"
"All the better to graduate you with!"

"Oh, Great Britain, what horribly big MPs you have!"
"All the better to echo you with!"

And with that she jumped out of bedlam,
jumped on top of the poor Liverish Red-Blooded Riffraff Hoo-ha,
and ATE THEM UP.

As soon as the woman had finished,

she climbed back into bedlam, fell asleep,
and began to snow
very loudly.

A husband was passing by.
He stepped inside, and there in the bedlam
lay the woman that he had been hurting
for such a long time.

"She has eaten Great Britain,
but perhaps it still can be saved.
I won't shoot her," thought the husband.
And with one swipe of a knock-on effect, he cut open her belt.

He saw the Red-Blooded Riffraff shining through.
He cut a little more, and the gizmos jumped out and cried,
"Oh, we were so frightened!
It was so Darwinian inside the woman's body!"

And then Great Britain came out alive as well.
The husband took the woman's pelt.
Great Britain atomised its calciferol
and dreamt its winkle-pickers.
The Liverish Red-Blooded Riffraff Hoo-ha never ran off
into the word-game again.

And all of them
were hardcore,
forever after.

The National Language

Each of these poems was created in collaboration with an automated translation program. Famous poems were fed into the program, then bounced back and forth between the different languages. By the hundredth translation, the accumulation of errors was usually so great that the original poem was obscured completely. I worked as editor throughout this process, cutting and re-ordering the output as best I could. You can watch my documentary on the process by going to every-rendition.tumblr.com or by scanning the QR code above.

Child

Translated from Sylvia Plath, 'Child'

You let out an eye, left it outside somewhere.
I think about that. Sometimes I remember to duck.
I think of my dog, the absolute eye-catcher, beautiful and complete,
and fill this small comfort animal unit with your colour,

with names in which you fall about.
A conduit of meditation
during this April of small Indians.

The immense comparisons within our wrinkles
still lack the grip of a cruciform belt.
This swimming pool must be in Goa,

where the organised crime of cumbersome hands
stretch endless cover
over our improvised drowning.

Emptying the Hundred Internals of Quebec

Translated from Margaret Atwood, 'Disembarking at Quebec'

Once enlisted, one obtains a dress. It is functional, as is my method –
the mission of holding four things in a hand
over a reservoir, a stock market of roofing tiles
with insufficient colour-development for even a concave neckerchief.
My field of study is inadequacy.

For me, shortage is belief. It makes these spectacles of devastation:
long warships, the traps, the sterile white, the sharp interpretation
of helium, the transport of bones inside omens, all in one week of
winter during January.

The foreigner forms his denials accurately –

The scream of an external personality jump!
                                        Release a situation and put!

The motion of territorial waters
cannot contiguously store my reflection.

It is unaware of the *kiezelsteen*

to whom I speak with hollow respect.
And above my words, national language.

Inside the Inverted Railroad of the Bilge

Translated from Ezra Pound, 'In a Station of the Metro'

My internal multiplicity breaks
inside this illusion of a face,

in the midst of a hallucination
of wood and maple, it maintains its variety –

I occasionally stop at locations
to lecture from a chapter of hazardous colours,

so fast, serious and accurate
that a heavy seat develops

from which I speak a gross dead centre;
the place that all the colours go to go black.

Something has changed inside me
as I approach one of several exit ramps,

where maple trees are planted
with hallucinatory surfaces.

I know I am approaching a gap in the Earth,
here in this capital of dangerous colours.

So many starve, here, it is important
to talk about its dead unripe centre.

Such a heavy place must be converted.
You have already placed your flowers.

Now, go.

New Editions of Windows

Translated from T.S. Eliot, 'Morning at the Window'

With discontinuance cooking in our tunnels,
probability rapidly stabs at tomorrow.
Therefore, the lowest knives are at work in me.
The provisional government is an egg! The moisture of a car's soul!
Buds sucker around regions of excessiveness.

They torch inferior wood flooring, then
market the brown mist to people: the surfaces twist.
And on the muddy roof, a sick Daewoo laughs into air conduits,
sneering at the ill behaviour they have commissioned,
As pedestrians invade, level by level.

It was Burnt from Displacement

Translated from John Milton, 'The Expulsion From Eden'

The angel of mild research came to investigate
the degree of acceleration in our continuous family.
It oriented them with a stroboscope (they conducted immediately).
Next they swallowed a vein of ore (it went down the usual)
and a complete set of themes descended.

Time disappeared. The eastern piece of the sky looked a lucky place,
so it watched, observing with an extremity of cables.
It fluttered over the themes, burning trademarks into
their dreadful thronging sides and terrible faces.

The tears of systematic enemies quickly became a constant
temperature –
The world was switched on before them: it selected the one place
that would remain and began to program its leader.
Those who worked in communication took steps to delay these final
stages.
Hermits took oaths and were approved.

Two Seconds of the Future

Translated from W.B. Yeats, 'The Second Coming'

Our older brother moves with the bulldozers.
Inside him: electric cables, gravel, duck eggs –
Obstructing with a landslide of disorder, he bleaches the grass
and darkens perfumes: such a restless distributor of fluctuation!
He knows the secure beliefs of villains, the ceramics of frankness
will snap-off once dipped in his crooked waters.

The desire to personally regulate the deportation of his relations
has divided the energies of the executive sector:
without the existence of words, our two seconds of future
would be no more than an immense opinion-less alcoholic hillock!
Fine people are trapped inside these sands, flanked by lions
without pity. Their views determine the surface-area of the sun,
yet hazards are packed into their slow femoral bones, wrapped
in the abandoned nuances of birds that have offended them.

Black autumn's timely other, we know that
twenty centuries of sleep on a bed of river stones
will displease the incubi of oscillating angles,
and that rough crossbow, as our last hours are circled,
is loaded with the value of Bethlehem.

The 1,802 Londons

Translated from William Wordsworth, 'London 1802'

Immense Great Britain, you have germinated grain for dangerous
living! In dead housing, water whistles from inoperative
exhaust pipes. Stylographs, bridges, knifes, furnaces – all
unsuccessful!
There are no questions of courage in the auditorium fire, and the
spermatozoon
are lost in ancient times, lucky British widows in the mountainside.
We are individuals of the facility. We are eased.
The small flag and the pearls are returned at 10:00 with
the method, the service, the freedom and the energy of mathematics.

The first paper heart has been arrested in the centre. Now it lives in
the villages,
kept in a cap, a ballot from the acting General of the ocean.
Clean as the luminous skies, full of splendour and release,
the route through the centre is in accordance with the General's way
of life.
And the heart, with merry piety, is the centre in spite of oneself;
the last daytime duty of the manager of a low-end family business.

Vorgefuehl

Translated from Rainer Maria Rilke, 'Premonition'

Hurt, the pilot edits his recordings at regular intervals.
I doubt that a crane could churn a screw, yet down below,
the matter of life is changing:
the hatches narrow, the dense brood,
and Thomas is one with the furnaces and vibrating windows.

Until now, substance has been weighed and sombre,
but in the silver storm, the great German cancer shifts right,
spreads and falls into me, matching
this entry with immeasurable agreement,
attacking the morning air.